First World War
and Army of Occupation
War Diary
France, Belgium and Germany

27 DIVISION
Divisional Troops
1/1 South Midland Field Company Royal Engineers
21 December 1914 - 30 April 1915

WO95/2258/4

The Naval & Military Press Ltd
www.nmarchive.com
Published in association with The National Archives

Published by

The Naval & Military Press Ltd

Unit 10 Ridgewood Industrial Park,

Uckfield, East Sussex,

TN22 5QE England

Tel: +44 (0) 1825 749494

www.naval-military-press.com

www.nmarchive.com

This diary has been reprinted in facsimile from the original. Any imperfections are inevitably reproduced and the quality may fall short of modern type and cartographic standards.

© **Crown Copyright**
Images reproduced by permission of The National Archives, London, England, 2015.

Contents

Document type	Place/Title	Date From	Date To
Heading	WO95/2258-4		
Heading	1/1st Sth Midland Fld Coy R.E. Dec 1914-Apr 1915 (Trans to 48th Divn 30.4.15)		
Heading	1st S. Midland Field Coy R.E. (27th Div) Vol I. 21.12.14-31.1.15		
War Diary		21/12/1914	31/01/1915
Heading	1st. Midland Field Coy R.E. (27th Divn) Vol II 1-28.2.15		
War Diary		01/02/1915	28/02/1915
Heading	1/1 S. Midland Field Coy R.E. Vol III 1-31.3.15		
War Diary		01/03/1915	31/03/1915
Heading	1st S. Midland Field Coy. R.E. Vol IV 1-30.4.15		
War Diary		01/04/1915	30/04/1915

3०५७/२२५८(4)

3०५७/२२५८(4)

27TH DIVISION
DIVL ENGINEERS

1/1ST STH MIDLAND FLD COY R.E.

DEC 1914 - APR 1915

(TRANS TO 48TH DIVN 30.4.'15)

M.T. 2
T.F. 1

121/4612

27th Division

1st S. Midland Field Coy RE. (27th Div)

Vol I. 21.12.14 — 31.1.15

Army Form C. 2118.

1st South Midland Field Coy. R.E.
29th Division

WAR DIARY
or
INTELLIGENCE SUMMARY

(Erase heading not required.)

Instructions regarding War Diaries and Intelligence Summaries are contained in F.S. Regs., Part II. and the Staff Manual respectively. Title pages will be prepared in manuscript.

Hour, Date, Place	Summary of Events and Information	Remarks and references to Appendices
10.15 a.m. 21.12.14	Marched from Winchester	Deficient of a great deal of our Mobilization Equipment. 9 G.S. wagons issued on 19th. 3 S.A.A. carts & forage carts. Any carts today were much on the G.S. wagon they would need considerable alteration for heavy loads. Not sufficient for Unloading heavy wagons: loaded & unloaded. Go there off & reloaded. Drew a quantity of our missing Equipment Owners & haute.
3.30 p.m.	Embarked at Southampton	
2 p.m. 22.12.14	Alongside Quay Havre	
11 p.m.	Completed disembarkation & marched to Rest Camp No. 1	
5.50 p.m. 23.12.14	Received orders to entrain at Joint No. 4 Gare de Marchandise at 6 am Dec 24th Entrainment completed	
10.19 a.m. 24.12.14	Arrived St Omer	
8 am 25.12.14	Detrainment completed & marched to Argues	
10.30 am	At Argues Engages on Defence line	Returned list of deficiencies on Platform. No counts started out a pattern about 10.20 for their troops very to hay. I had one extra wagon 16 a day with 1851 but nothing to follow. Mostly I'd made party filled in to attached copies of attached We hardly touched. Explanation was contained. It appears that particular pace to form up. they think they won't break to bother. Explanation was too late to...
Dec 25 & Jan 7	Port Rouge - 11.30 S of Revercoure also obstacles to Aviation ground for test by Artillery Fire & Machine fire Pic	

1247 W 3299 200,000 (E) 8/14 J.B.C. & A. Forms/C. 2118/11.

WAR DIARY or INTELLIGENCE SUMMARY

Army Form C. 2118.

2/1 South Midland Field Coy. R.E.
27th Division

Hour, Date, Place	Summary of Events and Information	Remarks and references to Appendices
Jan 5th 15	1 Coy. Inspected Pontoon Train at WITTES.	
- 6"	Pontoon left at WITTES with Divl Ammn Col. 3 Coys. Inspected the Centrifugal	
	Recd orders to move by train Jan 7th	
- 7"	Moved. Marches to MENNIS. 18 Drivers & 14 horses left at Argus isolated having been in contact with Scarlet Fever cases. Lieut Thomas in charge. Also Lieut Rueter as M.O. horse.	
Jan 8 8th	10 Drivers from No 95 Co A.S.C. Train &	
- 9"	9 do - No 98 Co Sent to enable unit to move	
- 10 th	Marches to 17" KOTCOELE Recennoitering at WESTOUTRE. Preparing for billets at Brewery Brandaye.	

Army Form C. 2118.

1st South Midland Field Coy R.E.
27th Division

WAR DIARY
or
INTELLIGENCE SUMMARY
(Erase heading not required.)

Hour, Date, Place	Summary of Events and Information	Remarks and references to Appendices
Jan 10th 15	D. on 9th Bn. supplies 72 Tels for use in Trenches. Tramways reported o/c breakdown on road on Jan 8th Repairs done by	
" 11	Road mending	Westoutre
" 12	do	do
" 13	d.	d.
" 14	d.	d. + Hutting Zevecoton
" 15	d.	d.
" 16	d.	d.
" 17	d.	d.
" 18	do	d.
Jan 19	Coy. squad moved to Zevecoton from Hdqrs at N.Hohenacke on Pontoons. Hutting Zevecoton. Fitting of Tramway at Dick & Burth for both etc. Road between Rudach & Pontoon crossed N. Hohenacke	

Army Form C. 2118.

1st South Midland Field Coy. R.E.
27th Division

WAR DIARY
or
INTELLIGENCE SUMMARY
(Erase heading not required.)

Instructions regarding War Diaries and Intelligence Summaries are contained in F. S. Regs., Part II. and the Staff Manual respectively. Title pages will be prepared in manuscript.

Hour, Date, Place	Summary of Events and Information	Remarks and references to Appendices
Jan 20 1915	3 Sections in Huts. 1 Section fitting up both Dickebusch Brewery	
21st 1915	do do do do	
22	do do do do	
23	do do do do	
24	Moved to Dickebusch	
	3 Sections in trenches repairs night. 1 out Davis. N° 1 Section put revetting front work hand bay/parapet across road by point at J.C101 1 out Savey. N° 2 Section improvement of parapet & range in B.3. 1 out Richard. N° 4 Section erecting m/c Trench on right of O.2. about 10 Jan & out flanker hand india [rapa?]/super dome [?] gun turret. O.E. put Dickebusch turn on & drains kept established at Vierstraat, La Brasserie & Voormezeele	
Jan 25	3 Sections in trenches night 25-26 & 1 out Davis N°1 Section improv. during D9. Remainder in rear [lent out?]	

1247 W 3299 200,000 (E) 8/14 J.B.C. & A. Forms/C. 2118/11.

Army Form C. 2118.

WAR DIARY
of
INTELLIGENCE SUMMARY
(Erase heading not required.)

1st South Midland Field Coy, R.E.
27th Division

Instructions regarding War Diaries and Intelligence Summaries are contained in F. S. Regs., Part II. and the Staff Manual respectively. Title pages will be prepared in manuscript.

Hour, Date, Place	Summary of Events and Information	Remarks and references to Appendices
Jan 26th	Night 25th – 26th 6th Jan Cont. Lieut Savory - N° 2 Section Continued work in B3. Capt Hoggson - N° 3 Section Continued work on right of B2. 3 Section in trenches night 26th - 27th Capt Hoggson - N° 3 Section Continued work on right of B2. Lieut Savory - N° 2 Section Continued work on N° 69. Lieut Richard - N° 4 Section Also Engagement Have now returned in reav. of 69 as drainage of redoubt & drainage 7 communication trenches in rear of C.8 partly carried out.	While at Dickebusch 3 Section found m.ts. trenches and right of flooding in about 5 f[t]— retaining about 1 am 1 Section found at work. Have to work in N.E. Red each day
Jan 27 G	3 Section in trenches & Night Jan 27th - 28th Capt Hoggson - N° 3 Section Continued work on right of B2. Lieut Dawn - N° 1 Section Continued work on C9 drainage + widening had they ent, & there already made to be taken	

1247 W 3299 200,000 (E) 8/14 J.B.C. & A. Forms/C. 2118/11.

Army Form C. 2118.

1st South Midland Field Coy R.E.
29th Division

WAR DIARY
or
INTELLIGENCE SUMMARY
(Erase heading not required.)

Instructions regarding War Diaries and Intelligence Summaries are contained in F. S. Regs., Part II. and the Staff Manual respectively. Title pages will be prepared in manuscript.

Hour, Date, Place	Summary of Events and Information	Remarks and references to Appendices
Jan 27-15 Cont'd	Night 27th - 28th Cont'd. Lieut Richards & N°4 Section Engineers cont'd drainage on Redoubt at J. Kroi	
Jan 28th. 15.	Night 28-29th 3 Section in trenches Lieut Dann & N°1 Section continued work in trenches E.9. Dressing stations & improving dugouts Lieut Sarony, N°2 Section to B4. improving parapet, building traverse, Junction Lieut Richards N°4 Section laying parapet on J2 also Junction J1 J2 Lieut. Relved in night of J.2.	
Jan 29th 15	Night 29th - 30th Lieut Dann N°1 Section cont'd in C.9 Cont'd Shrub improvements & Comm'n trench Lieut Sarony N°2 Section. Making strong point in Bois (Influence) Section 8"	

1247 W 3299 200,000 (E) 8/14 J.B.C.& A. Forms/C. 2118/11.

Army Form C. 2118.

1st South Midland Field Coy R.E.
29th Division

WAR DIARY
or
INTELLIGENCE SUMMARY
(Erase heading not required.)

Instructions regarding War Diaries and Intelligence Summaries are contained in F. S. Regs., Part II. and the Staff Manual respectively. Title pages will be prepared in manuscript.

Hour, Date, Place	Summary of Events and Information	Remarks and references to Appendices
Jan 29.15 Cmd	Night 29th-30th Cmd. Capt Hosegood, Mr Blacker Relieving Strong point in BOIS CARRÉ Went delayed thro' Infantry party being & must [?]	
Jan 30.15	Night 30-31st Capt Hosegood & No 3 Cmd Strong point in Bois Carré Lieut Savory No 2 Sec Out Shoppen Bois Commune Lieut Michane No 1 Sec Cmd West in L9 ? 1/Hoteproofs in Ommer Trench Morts 6 ZENITHUTON	
Jan 31.15		

1247 W 3299 200,000 (E) 8/14 J.B.C. & A. Forms/C. 2118/11.

097
8PM
M.T.2
T.F.1

121/4612

27th Division

1st Lowland Field Coy R.E. (27th Div")

Vol II 1-28.2.15

WAR DIARY or INTELLIGENCE SUMMARY

Army Form C. 2118.

1st South Midland Field Coy R.E.
27th Division

Hour, Date, Place	Summary of Events and Information	Remarks and references to Appendices
Feb. 1 . 15.	1 Section working on Road WIELTJE to ST. JULIEN. 1 Section filled in bad holes on ZEVECOTEN - ZONNEBEKE Road & prepared for piering 28th Division. Rest of Company resting at ZEVECOTEN. Had trouble trying for 40 men to fit bags & 1 Sapper ends. 9ft high parapet reft. of 6"x 4" timber every foot. Lines with 6"x 1" rough boards sawn to width. Everything is far as available. Everything for heavier than necessary but all that was available. Three sections were going well could turn out & have for day. Hule covered with roofing felt. We also provided tar engine driver for both at BOESCHEPE. 1 Carpenter & Corporal of Majors Bevonage and Carpenter & Plumber at Batty DICKEBUSCH. 3 Section to stick , on Road above Indian labor employed on Road about 90 men per day gave 3f look.	
Feb 2nd 15.	3 Section on Hut & latrine on Road also No. 4 & 5 Coys Belg. or Artillery Station west on Road from LOCRE to DICKEBUSCH church. Even Engineers.	
– 3 15		

Army Form C. 2118.

1st South Midland Field Coy. R.E.
27th Division

WAR DIARY
INTELLIGENCE SUMMARY
(Erase heading not required.)

Instructions regarding War Diaries and Intelligence Summaries are contained in F. S. Regs., Part II. and the Staff Manual respectively. Title pages will be prepared in manuscript.

Hour, Date, Place	Summary of Events and Information	Remarks and references to Appendices
Feb 3rd 15 cont	R.E. working at RENINGHELST & billets with Inf. Hall in charge	
Feb 4th 15.	3 Sections Hutting. 1 Section on Road	
— 5th 14	2 do. do. 2 do. do.	
— 6. 15	1 Section Hutting 2 Section on Road	
	1 Section working with No 4 0/1758/y in billets on road.	
Feb 7th 14	2 Sections on tent. 2 Section on Road	
Feb 8th 15	Moved to DICKEBUSCH to take over Right hand section	This is where I took over this Diary on left by Major Gardiner killed Mar 2. 1915.
Feb. 9.	3 Sections working in trenches – 2 parties supervising Belgian road repairing – Hauling bricks to roads with turnurodecant. 2 Timber from BAILLEUL –	
Feb.10.	3 Sections in Trenches – dugouts & wire entanglements. Mortar emplacement in Trench Mob. stores – 2 parties roadmaking – Timber & brick hauling –	
Feb. 11.	2 Sections in Trenches & dugouts – 5 Hut. stables for Dressing station – Bricks & road repairing – 2 men working at BREWERY at Vlam – Sergt of No 4 Section fatally shot on R. section –	

Army Form C. 2118.

1st South Midland Field Coy. R.E.
29th Division

WAR DIARY

INTELLIGENCE SUMMARY

(Erase heading not required.)

Instructions regarding War Diaries and Intelligence Summaries are contained in F. S. Regs., Part II. and the Staff Manual respectively. Title pages will be prepared in manuscript.

Hour, Date, Place	Summary of Events and Information	Remarks and references to Appendices
Sept 12. 1915.	Hut for Camp Commandant started near R.E. Hd Qrs. Hospital hut proceeded with. 1 Section on R & on L sections respectively. A redoubt started behind No 4 Trench - a dugouts repairs which adjacent thereto.	
" 13.1915.	Hospital hut completed. C.C's hut completed. Our night 1 Section proceeded with works on the Mound on R section and 1 section worked out, where 1 sapper was reported missing and two were wounded and detained at Hospital.	
" 14.1915.	Road repairs during the day and preparing site for mortuary. Working RE Barm. All sections stood by at night and at 5AM proceeded to dig on 2nd line.	
" 15.1915.	At 10 AM. 4 sappers were killed. 1 Corpl wounded - (severely by a high explosive shell. And 1 sapper wounded on R of second line - Company returned to billets at noon. Two sections working on R & L sections respectively - rectifying and repairing trenches and on Mound in R section.	
" 16.1915.	Road work. Mortuary hut and road repairing proceeded. 2 sections were working - one on R & one on L. sections.	

1247   W 3299   200,000   (E)   8/14   J.B.C. & A.   Forms/C. 2118/11.

WAR DIARY
INTELLIGENCE SUMMARY

Army Form C. 2118.

1st South Midland Field Coy. R.E.
27th Division

Hour, Date, Place	Summary of Events and Information	Remarks and references to Appendices
Feb. 17. 1914.	Working as usual. Sapper previously reported missing on morning of 15th now reported killed. 2 sappers at BREWERY heating arrangements. 2 Section working on R & L Sections.	
Feb. 18. 1914.	R.E. PARK roadway repairs. 1 Section on L & 1 on R section. a second hut started for C. Commandant. Timber houses from BAILLEUL.	
Feb. 19. 1914.	Road repairs – hauling bricks – hut proceeded with. One section ditto(?) arrangements on L & one section working on hound R section. One sapper to POORMEZEELE to repair pumps – 2 & appers on water supply in DICKIE BUSCH.	
Feb. 20. 1915.	2 Sections on L & R section – on L section Sergt Nº1 section were wounded and 1 sapper also wounded. During the day parties were out road repairing etc.	
Feb. 21. 1915.	2 Sections in firing line. Redoubt 1 completely ruined, Mound had the french construction at back – a dugouts made throughout the day & night.	
Feb. 22. 1915.	A new Redoubt was made in BOIS DE CONFLUENCE near trench S.6. During day work as usual. The 2 sections on R & L respectively were employed in Trenches and on new Redoubt – on coming out of the Trenches after work, 1 sapper was wounded	
Feb. 23. 1914.	Work as usual in R.E. Park – road repairing as usual in the morning. All carts packed and at NOON the Company left for ZEVECOTEN arriving at about 3 P.M. The various parties left behind to hand over billets and work followed on and all were in by 7 P.M.	

Army Form C. 2118.

1st South Midland Coy RE
29th Division

WAR DIARY
or
INTELLIGENCE SUMMARY
(Erase heading not required.)

Instructions regarding War Diaries and Intelligence Summaries are contained in F. S. Regs., Part II. and the Staff Manual respectively. Title pages will be prepared in manuscript.

Hour, Date, Place	Summary of Events and Information	Remarks and references to Appendices
Feb 24.19.15.	Two sappers proceeded to Beauchamp Blumery to manage its waterplant for huts. One section instructed a squad. A party repaired existing huts. One section started a colony of huts on KIMNELL Road - with civilian assistance - Road repairs were carried out by civil labour under R.E. supervision. Sand - bricks - hoppers were hauled and timber for huts. One section proceeded to VLAMERTINGHE when they built and built huts - a motor lorries for 28 div.	
Feb 25.19.15.	Whole section worked - and same programme was carried out.	
Feb 26.19.15.	Hutting and drainage were proceeded with at both places. A swan bridge was repaired by one section. One section rating - standing for road waters - Section at VLAMERTINGHE returned to billets at ZEVECOTEN warning.	
Feb 27.19.15.	A fresh section proceeded to VLAMERTINGHE to carry on hutting, the other three sections were employed on local hutting, draining wood and matting a previous roadway to huts.	
Feb 28.19.15.	One section hutting & matting - 2 were proceeded to Beauchamp to repair pumps. Remainder employed on usual errands etc. Huts occupied.	

CB Hargood Capt.
O.C. S.M. 2d.C. RE.

1311/48/4

24th Divn

1/1 S Midland Fd Coy RE.

Vol III 1 - 31.3.15

Army Form C. 2118.

WAR DIARY
INTELLIGENCE SUMMARY
(Erase heading not required.)

1/1st South Midland Field Company R.E. (Y.4)

Hour, Date, Place	Summary of Events and Information	Remarks and references to Appendices
Mar 1. 1915	Packed up carts at ZEVECOTEN, and in the morning, proceeded to NEW HUTS at DICKIEBUSCH at NOON. One section stayed back at huts to hand over to 2nd Wsx. R.E. Team. It was arranged that two sections should do the work in the trenches for two consecutive nights and then have two nights not, unless unforeseen circumstances should demand more sections out at the same time – ALLWOOD's or L section for the 12 days period. The two sections went out at 6 P.M and were joined later by O.C. Some trenches were temporarily untakken by our infantry accompanied by the sappers and men of the heavy firing Major Gardiner and Lt Davis went off to look after a missing party, and while doing so Major Gardiner was fatally shot while outside trench No 21. It was not possible to recover his body as the enemy were making a successful counter attack – just beyond this trench a party of our sappers were working and 1 Sapper was killed and 1 Corporal was wounded and later found to be missing. Lt Davis was also reported missing.	Lt B.O. Bunting transferred to us from 2nd Wsx. Fd.C. R.E.
Mar 2.	Our sections working on articles to take to the trenches at night and 5 men were prematurely told off for duty with Major SANKEY on 2nd Mar. Bricks were hauled to trenches, who were repairing MILLCRUYSRoad	

1247 W 3299 300,000 (E) 8/14 J.B.C. & A. Forms/C. 2118/11.

Army Form C. 2118.

WAR DIARY
of
INTELLIGENCE SUMMARY

(Erase heading not required.) 1/1st South Midland Field Company R.E. (4.9)

Instructions regarding War Diaries and Intelligence Summaries are contained in F. S. Regs., Part II. and the Staff Manual respectively. Title pages will be prepared in manuscript.

Hour, Date, Place	Summary of Events and Information	Remarks and references to Appendices
Mar. 2. 1915.	Usual R.E. supervision – 2 Storekeepers installed at R.E. PARK VOORMEZEELE.	
Mar. 3. 1915.	Day work proceeded in the R.E. Park as usual – and bricks were hauled to roads under repair – No Davies not missing but wounded in face. Sent to hospital now Boulogne. Trenches were repaired after the 5 hour bombardment of the German front line. L. section – one corpl. and three sappers attached to park during the time Company at here. – Two sappers were also attached to BREWERY during remainder of Company's stay here.	The sections are very seriously impaired in numbers by casualties and its drawing on them for good men for semi-permanent jobs.
Mar. 4.	2 Sections on work in Park – and in driving up in Trenches. A new trench was dug W of Maund in L section – while the wet weather lasts nothing much can be done in this line.	
Mar. 5.	Day work as usual. While the bricks were being loaded on waggon DICKIEBUSCH – YPRES road shrapnel fire killed one – wounded seven Maund trench carried on as usual.	Very few sound H. Draught horses left.
Mar. 6.	One horse wounded yesterday, shot. R.E. Park work carried on as usual.	
Mar. 7.	Work carried on in CRIMEA TRENCH – drainage – digging to connect up with No. 14. Wire entanglements laid outside. Usual routine during the day. Traffic control to ordnance stores added owing to H.E. shells fired near LA CLYTTE.	

1247 W 3299 200,000 (E) 8/14 J.B.C.&A. Forms/C. 2118/11.

Army Form C. 2118.

WAR DIARY
or
INTELLIGENCE SUMMARY

(Erase heading not required.) 1/1st South Midland Field Company RE (44)

Instructions regarding War Diaries and Intelligence Summaries are contained in F. S. Regs., Part II. and the Staff Manual respectively. Title pages will be prepared in manuscript.

Hour, Date, Place	Summary of Events and Information	Remarks and references to Appendices
Mar. 8. 1915.	1 NCO & 1 Sapper on all day revised & night for making a dugout for artillery. 2 Sections loading & preparing stores in park. At night two sections carrying on at CRIMEA TRENCH and reporting on R.B. Trench in front. Were returning & carried forward & placed for 110ᵡ. Hope to have 50ᵡ fire trench two tomorrow O.C. Lincolnshire interviewed.	Short of establishment. Officers 2, Sappers 33, Drivers 7
Mar. 9. 1915.	All day bombardment of enemy front & 2nd line with our H.E. howitzers. Left Bruce with O.C. R.B. to go up in evening with first party. Artillery dugout not finished two men supplied. Very active night. 2 Sections on Crimea trench - drainage & communication trench with Reserve - 1 Off. 2 men sent to Trench 17 to sap forward to Saffell with a short demolished sap reconnoitred & sap to Trench No.18. This was started. Bricks hauled in country carts. Went in Park by 2 sections. - 3 Tool carts Toftrm one a pair of in lieu of those damaged. Two sections with 3 Officers out at night. Two parties of 1 Officer 1 NCO & 2 Sappers each, started from Trenches 17 & 18 respectively to link up. Not much progress made. - 2 NCOs sent to Pencethoret to superintend drawing & revettt to facilitate a sap to be linking No.19 to form a new trench - in view of No.19. Balance of section under 1 officer continued wiring and drainage between Crimea & No.14 Trench. 1 NCO & 2 men making new dugout for R.A. staff. - 2 Sections of Sappers in Park matting.	
Mar. 10. 1915		
Mar. 11. 1915.	Suitable for the nights work. Bridge & road hauled to curtain road reserves. on going through YOORMEZEELE on the way up to Trenches 1 man was shot through the knee. Working parties consisted of: Improving communication between S.9 and S.7, laying flooring and draining efforts at intervals. The wire entanglements along this front were frightfully annoys and opening kept at intervals.	
Mar. 12. 1915.	The NCO and two men were continuing this sap in No.17. 2 Sections in Park. 2 sections in Trenches at night. Work carried on as before in Crimea district. This was too late right of our 12 day period. Drivers hauled bricks in the morning and cleared up and packed later.	

1247 W 8299 200,000 (E) 8/14 J.B.C. & A. Forms/C. 2118/11.

Army Form C. 2118.

WAR DIARY
or
INTELLIGENCE SUMMARY

(Erase heading not required.) 1/1st South Midland Field Company RE (44)

Instructions regarding War Diaries and Intelligence Summaries are contained in F.S. Regs., Part II. and the Staff Manual respectively. Title pages will be prepared in manuscript.

Hour, Date, Place	Summary of Events and Information	Remarks and references to Appendices
Mar. 13. 1915.	2 Sections in Park – 1 NCO & 2 men finishing R.A. dugout – 2 Engineers or Beauchamp Brassin – More. The Company moved back to that billets at ZEVECOTEN at 12.30 P.M. Two sick horses were left behind I/c of a man – ZEVECOTEN reached 2.30 and billets taken over. Horses billeted still at Brassine. Settled in & took our work from 2nd W Sx 2d Co RE who took over our billets. Paid 1/00 F to Belgian for billets	To Z EVECOTEN Read billets
Mar. 14. 1915.	All sappers available at work on huts at CANADA HOUSE Fr. Horses groomed & harness looked to & cleaned. At 9 o'clock rec'd a wire to hold ourselves ready to move at a moments notice. All horses harnessed up – a man in machine gun wire until 4 A.M. At 8 o'clock we were ordered to continue ordinary work on huts. Sent out 2 sections Rested one. Kept one in for Instructing Infantry in sapping. At 1.30 P.M. Königstr. turned up. Tkpt was the clearly packed up. NCO Kpning waterproofs at Battn.	
Mar. 15/9/14.	2 Sections hutting, one sapping instruction – 1 resting & bathing – Horses out on full or picket line. Drew 8 good L.D. horses from Boeschaepe. Paid section.	
Mar. 16.	2 Sections out – I resting & bathing – At 10.30 A.M. rec'd wire to prepare to move (including pontoons) Drew 2 L.D. horses Boeschaepe. Called in working sections prepared to move. Heard at 1.30 P.M. no move until 8 A.M. tomorrow. Paid 3 sections & drivers, when all preparations for move were complete.	Mon to MONT NOIR
Mar. 17.	The company moved to MONT NOIR, Starting 8 A.M. – After halting two sections with two Section 57st 2d C RE moved to KEMMEL – as a composite Coy – known as S.M. 2d C. The two remaining sections with the other two 57st sections manned MONT NOIR as 57st 2d C. – Both Companies attached to III Div. The S.M. 2d C. – marched out a conc; trench from LATERIE to S.S Redoubt.	Transferred from 27th to 3rd Div.

1247 W 3290 200,000 (E) 8/14 J.B.C. & A. Forms/C. 2118/11.

Army Form C. 2118.

WAR DIARY
or
INTELLIGENCE SUMMARY

(Erase heading not required.) 1/1st South Midland Field Company R.E. (Y.Y)

Instructions regarding War Diaries and Intelligence Summaries are contained in F. S. Regs, Part II. and the Staff Manual respectively. Title pages will be prepared in manuscript.

Hour, Date, Place	Summary of Events and Information	Remarks and references to Appendices
May 18.	S.M. 2d Co. (Capt Hassyed O.C.) marched out further down trench, whilst 57th (O.C. Major Howard R.E.) visited in back billets.	
May 19.	S.M. 2d Co. Sent 1 section into KEMMEL to obtain wood for entanglements from old houses. Supervised infantry (a Coy.) digging comn: trench previously marked out. 57th sections – making stakes – cutting brushwood & pickets.	
May 20.	Do. Do.	
May 21.	S.M. sections continued supervising infantry completing comn. trench. 57 Section cuttings & hauling pickets to KEMMEL for entanglements.	
May 22.	S.M. made wire entanglement – drew S. African queen – from S to road near J.11. 57 Co. same as day before.	
May 23.	Changed villup – from KEMMEL to MONT NOIR.	
May 24.	S M Coy noted & changed up – 57 2d Co. noted to billets – and prepared quick-meeting to trenches. The two companies again separated 57th to IIIrd Div S.M. to remain in coy H.Q. at St Eloi. Transferred to V Div.	Transferred to V Div 14 Inf Bgde. Separate from 57 M.C.
May 25.	Section # 3 & 4 took 1st lift at KEMMEL for four days & night – No horses or transport remained at KIMMEL – Rations every evening by ration cart from MONT NOIR. Sappers were split up into 16 different parties to supervise and assist infantry to improve trenches. Nos 102 sections making stakes & hurdles. Horses were clipped & all harness inspected – O.C. rode round trenches with Brigadier. Same work proceeded as day before – but found work too scattered to supervise properly.	

Army Form C. 2118.

WAR DIARY
or
INTELLIGENCE SUMMARY

(Erase heading not required.) 1/1st South Midland Field Coy -RE (44)

Instructions regarding War Diaries and Intelligence Summaries are contained in F. S. Regs., Part II. and the Staff Manual respectively. Title pages will be prepared in manuscript.

Hour, Date, Place	Summary of Events and Information	Remarks and references to Appendices
Mar 26.	Same sections on day before in same places. Infantry moved up to trench work unable to do it without outside aid. (i) Started on repairing J.3. by supplying between 50ps to connect up and J3 L with J3 R (60') and improving parapet. (ii) Started new Support behind G2. Casualty. 1 Sapper wounded in jaw over own (iii) Started improving new Trench G4 A in front of G4. with two platoons infantry. Same work proceeded as before. on G4 A - G2 S at J.3. at J.3. dt. Bunting wounded shoulder was bad spot.	
Mar 27		
Mar 28	Reliefs changed. Same work carried on - pickets being cut a hand by parties wagons to KEMMEL- work on J3 L abandoned & delaying of placing up two gap of 4' each taken on - trifling up unto sandbags.	
Mar 29.	Same work as previous days - 1 Sapper wounded in hip at 6.15 -	
Mar 30	Same work at both places - 1 Sapper wounded in finger at G2 S.	
Mar 31	Reliefs changed. Lt Bunting to Hospital BAILLEUL leaving Capt Hossgard & 2/Lt Richards a 2/Lt Seavey as officers. Same work as before.	

CB Hossgard Capt.
O.C. S. Md G. Fd Co.
Apl 2 - 1915-

131/5108

27th Div.

1st S. Midland Field Coy. R.E.

Vol IV 1 - 30.4.15.

Army Form C. 2118.

WAR DIARY
or
INTELLIGENCE SUMMARY
(Erase heading not required.)

Instructions regarding War Diaries and Intelligence Summaries are contained in F. S. Regs., Part II. and the Staff Manual respectively. Title pages will be prepared in manuscript.

Hour, Date, Place	Summary of Events and Information	Remarks and references to Appendices
Sept 1.	Relief changed – 2/Lt Savory wounded man. G.I.S. leaving Capt Honeysett & 2/Lt Richards.	
Sept 2.	Later in day 2/Lt Tapp, 2/Lt Le Cpt and 48 men arrived from old camp RODEN. Draft composed of 1 Officer – 1 N.C.O 38 Sappers 10 drivers. Occupied drivers and sapping men draft to 2 sections.	Draft arrived under 2/Lt Tapp –
Sept 3.	Work in KEMMEL as before. pickets out and hauled in pontoon waggons to KEMMEL PARK from MONT NOIR. Turly draft up to KEMMEL in evening to work for an hour in safe trenches. 1 N.C.O of new draft wounded coming down again. Draft and two sections at KEMMEL returned at dawn to MONT NOIR and rested during the next day.	
Sept 4.	Company rested for first part of day, except old portion of sections #4 & #2 who had not been to KEMMEL the day before – These men cut pickets and started them for hauling. Late in the afternoon received orders to proceed to YPRES at NOON. Rectified rest day. Packed waggons and cleared up camp and billets.	Ordered to YPRES under 28 D.N.
Sept 5.	Cleared camp and drew up outside MONT NOIR with concealing orders to proceed to YPRES. Noon for YPRES at 12-1 PM. received – returned to billets – ordered to hold ourselves in readiness for a move.	
Sept 6.	Recd. wire to move to MERRIS under So.Mid.Div. Moved off at 11.15 AM. Arrived at 3 PM via St JEANCAPELLE - METERIN – Short of horses. No spares –	Move to MERRIS under S.M.Div.

1247 W 3209 200,000 (E) 8/14 J.B.C.&A. Forms/C. 2118/11.

WAR DIARY or INTELLIGENCE SUMMARY

Army Form C. 2118.

(Erase heading not required.)

Instructions regarding War Diaries and Intelligence Summaries are contained in F. S. Regs., Part II. and the Staff Manual, respectively. Title pages will be prepared in manuscript.

1st S. MIDLAND FIELD CO. R.E., T.F.

Hour, Date, Place	Summary of Events and Information	Remarks and references to Appendices
Apl 7.	Took Sappers to 12. Coy do PAILLE when No 2 Coy and S.M. Du. R.E. Hd. Qrs. were billeted. Sent two sappers to Hd Qrs for R.E. work. Portion of R.E. Hd Qrs consisting of M.O. Instructors – and drivers for six horses – four mules returned and billeted with us –	
Apl 8.	Sappers putting up horse-shelter. Kit inspection and deficiency rebuts put through. Another move to VII Div indicated for 10th inst. 1 horse died - 1 cart, 1 Pattern over by Vet hosp. – 11 D.2. horses inducted for.	
Apl 9.	Orders to proceed to ERQUINGHEM on 10th inst. Sappers engaged in packing up stores – and building stalls from old shelters lying near – Drivers returned horses and prepared for the move. Visited J.O.C.S.M.D.	
Apl 10.	Moved to ERQUINGHEM – under Gloss a Worcester Bgde. Arrived 6 PM and troop over billets – stalls and Park received by 1st London 2d Co R.E. Booked by Capt Campbell. Adjutant – 4th London 2d Co who handed over.	Move to ERQUINGHEM. Attached to VI Div.
Apl 11.	Cleaned up billets – park etc. – visited Capt Kemp C.R.E. – and started to organise PARK. Coy went to Church Parade. visited London Coy.	
Apl 12.	Arranged to draw timber – visited yards – Gen Gordon 19 Bgde. and 12 Coy R.E. under whom we work at present. Some stores arrived at PARK and we took over patterns of work from 4th London Coy R.E.	
Apl 13.	Wagons hauled timber – 2 men from each section visited huts at GRIS POT to learn methods of construction – Took over explaining for bridge and fitted up boxes. Put up pontoon bridge.	
Apl 14.	Wagon hauling timber – work carried on in yard – Pontooning practice. Night work on communication trenches	Major W. Clissold arriving also 2 Lt M.W.J. Freeman.

1247 W 3299 200,000 (17) 8/14 J.B.C. & A. Forms/C. 2118/11.

WAR DIARY or INTELLIGENCE SUMMARY

Army Form C. 2118.

1st S. MIDLAND FIELD CO.
R.E., T.F.

Hour, Date, Place	Summary of Events and Information	Remarks and references to Appendices
Apl 15	Wagon hauling timber PC – 2 Section pontooning, 1 section working at night on communication trench.	1018 S. Green wounded (2nd time) 1218 A.D. Godfrey wounded
Apl 16	Wagon as before – 2 sections pontooning – one section night work on communication trench.	
Apl 17	Two sections moved to forward billet at BOIS GRENIER to facilitate work. The other forms details for work in yard & practices pontooning. Wagon hauling.	
Sunday Apl 18	The whole company had baths at girls' bathing place. Civilian labour was arrived in yard up to 6.2 pm also hauling. The Company took over the supply of the 19th Infy Bde with Engineering Stores re from the 72nd Field Coy R.E. Work in yard & on trenches. Boat making begun.	
Apl 19	Branch communication trench on Right begun.	2nd Lt. J.B. Watling joined the Coy.
Apl 20	Work on 2nd line begun at CROIX BALOT	
Apl 21	"	
Apl 22	"	
Apl 23	"	
Apl 24	SOS bomb completed – Circular saw installed in Yard. Section in forward billet changed.	
Sunday Apl 25	Civilian labour and hauling as usual. Men not employed attended Divine Service. Circular saw installed in yard.	
Apl 26	Work in Yard & Bomb construction & on trenches continued.	
Apl 27	Civilian party of 43 worked at night at RATION Farm	

WAR DIARY or **INTELLIGENCE SUMMARY**
(Erase heading not required.)

Army Form C. 2118.

Hour, Date, Place	Summary of Events and Information	Remarks and references to Appendices
April 28	Work in yards — Boat making — Night work — Trenches. Total number of civilians employed 303 — Rate during week 3/- per man.	
	3/- Ihour in Trenches top of — Night work 7hour on trenches 5/- Civilians worked at night.	
April 29	As on 28th. All civilian parties got to work by night.	
April 30	Orders received for transfer to S.M. Davis & handing over to 12th Field Coy.	

J.W. Chissold
Major RE(T)

www.ingramcontent.com/pod-product-compliance
Lightning Source LLC
Chambersburg PA
CBHW081503160426
43193CB00014B/2578